The
Singing Green

The Singing Green

New *and Selected Poems*
for All Seasons

Eve Merriam

ILLUSTRATED BY
Kathleen Collins Howell

MORROW JUNIOR BOOKS
NEW YORK

Library of Congress Cataloging-in-Publication Data
Merriam, Eve.
The singing green / by Eve Merriam; illustrated by
Kathleen Collins Howell.   p.   cm.
Summary: An illustrated collection of poems on a variety of topics.
ISBN 0-688-11025-8 (trade).
1. Children's poetry, American.   [1. American poetry.]
I. Howell, Kathleen Collins, ill.   II. Title.
PS3525.E639S58   1992
811'.54—dc20   91-31205   CIP   AC

For Janet
with loving friendship
in every season

CONTENTS

SALLIES
AND
SAUNTERS

SUMMER RAIN

A shower, a sprinkle,
a tangle, a tinkle,
greensilver runs the rain.

Like salt on your nose,
like stars on your toes,
tingles the tangy rain.

A tickle, a trickle,
a million-dot freckle
speckles the spotted rain.

Like a cinnamon
geranium
smells the summertime rain!

A VOTE FOR VANILLA

Vanilla, vanilla, vanilla for me,
that's the flavor I savor particularly
in cake or ice cream
or straight from the bean
in pudding, potatoes, in fish or in stew,
in a sundae, a Monday, the whole week-long through!

I care not a sou, a hoot, or scintilla,
a fig or a farthing—except for vanilla!
Boo, phoo, eschew sarsaparilla;
more, adore, encore vanilla!
From the Antarctic to the Antilles,
Viva Vanilles!

On the first of Vanilla I'll write to you,
at half-past vanilla we'll rendezvous;
by the light of vanilla we'll dance and we'll fly
until vanilla dawns in the sky.
Then to a vanilla villa we'll flee
by the vanilla side of the sea,
with vanilla tables, vanilla chairs,
vanilla carpeting on the stairs,
vanilla dogs, vanilla cats,
vanilla shoes, vanilla hats,
vanilla mice in vanilla holes,
vanilla soup in vanilla bowls:

vanilla, vaniller, vanillest for me,
the flavor I favor most moderately!

WHO'S HERE?

Here's a curmudgeon.
What is he wearing?
He has a grudge on.

Is he down in the dumps?
Is he feeling low?
No.
He's in a high dudgeon.

It's hard to make a *j*
sound anything but joyful:
it's jubilant, it's jocund,
it joins in a jig.
It japes, it jibes, it jingles,
it jitterbugs, it jets.
It jangles, it jumps rope,
it jounces in a jeep.
It jiggles, it joggles,
it's juicy, it's jam-full,
it's a jester, a jockey,
a jaunty jackanapes.
It's a juggler, a jouster,
a jar full of jelly beans,
it's a julep, a jujube,
a jocose jinni,
a journey in a jolly boat—

by jeepers, by jiminy,
by Juno and by Jupiter,
what jovial high jinks!

ANIMALIMERICKS

1. *Beware!*

When a cub, unaware being bare
was the best-dressed state for a bear,
put on a barrel
for wearing apparel:
his mother cried, "This I can't bear!"

2. *An Odd One*

There once was a finicky ocelot
who all the year round was cross a lot
except at Thanksgiving,
when he enjoyed living,
for he liked to eat cranberry sauce a lot.

3. *Variety*

A chameleon, when he's feeling blue,
can alter his glum point of view
by changing his hue
to a color that's new:
I'd like to do that, wouldn't you?

CHEERS

The frogs and the serpents each had a football team.
and I heard their cheerleaders in my dream:

"Bilgewater, bilgewater," called the frog.
"Bilgewater, bilgewater,
sis, boom, bog!
Roll 'em off the log,
slog 'em in the sog,
swamp 'em, swamp 'em,
muck mire quash!"

"Sisyphus, Sisyphus," hissed the snake.
"Sibilant, syllabub,
syllable-loo-ba-lay.
Scylla and Charybdis,
sumac, asphodel,
how do you spell Success!
With an S-S-S!"

THE DREADFUL DRAWKCAB

It's live and evil,
it will step on pets,
set part of a trap,
stab at bats,
turn a star
into rats.

GRUMP

Grump grump grump grump
grump grump grouse:
where will you find
the grouch's house?

Grouse grouse grouse grouse
grump grump grump:
look underneath
the oak tree stump.

Far below the mushrooms
hear the grouch mumble:
grump grouse grunt grunt
grumble grumble grumble.

T V

In the house
of Mr. and Mrs. Spouse
he and she
would watch TV
and never a word
between them spoken
until the day
the set was broken.

Then "How do you do?"
said he to she.
"I don't believe
that we've
met
yet.
Spouse is my name.
What's yours?" he asked.

"Why, mine's the same!"
said she to he,
"Do you suppose that we could be—?"

But the set came suddenly right about,
and so they never did find out.

CIRCUS TIME

The circus is coming to town!
The brass band plays OOmpah OOmpah
thumpa thump
thumpa THUMP
thumpa OOmpah OOmpah *pow.*
Get your ticket
get your ticket
the Big Show's beginning right *now.*
Get your popcorn
get your program
get your root beer and frankfurter here.
The tent goes up goes *up* goes UP,
the sawdust ring is spread,
get a grandstand seat—hey, *down* in front,
we can't see over your head!
The lions growl in their cages,
the tamer cracks his whip,
oompah thump   oompah thump
the bears dance, the elephants prance,
oompah thump   oompah thump
a poodle pulls a cart with a cat,
a rabbit jumps from a black top hat,
a parakeet whistles "Dixie"
and drinks from a paper cup.
Thumpa thump.
Trapezes fly, your heart goes skip
as a bicycle climbs the high wire
oompah thump   oompah *thump.*
Acrobats tumble and leapfrog,

spangles and tightropes and spotlights,
a leotard lady, a leopard-skin man,
and a giant baby who lifts a van
OOOMP!
And watch him fall down, the comical clown
with the conical hat and the pom-poms
the chalk-white cheeks and the cherry-red nose
and the horn that blows
and the hidden hose
that squirts water wherever he goes.
Honk!
The circus is coming to town.
OOmpah *honk*!
The circus is coming to town.
HONK!

OUT OF THE CITY

"Eugene,"
said Claire,
"let's drive somewhere
and picnic in the open air."

"Keen,"
said Eugene,
"the air will be clean,
and the grass will be green."

So they drove
and they drove
and they drove and they drove
and they drove and they drove
and they drove
        and they drove
until they found
some open ground
where they hurried and ate
because it was late
and then turned the car around

and they drove
and they drove
and they drove
and they drove

and they drove
and they drove
and they drove
and they drove
back from the clean
green
scene.

A RHYME IS A JUMP ROPE

A rhyme is a jump rope, let's begin.
Take a turn and jump right in.

What can we do with a rhyme for today?
There are lots of chime-words we can say.
It might be fun to sail in the bay.
If there's a wind, the mast will sway.
If a storm comes up, the clouds will be gray.
The month of April begins with an A.
The month after that is known as May.
There's a bird that's blue that's called a jay.
In Paris there's a street named Rue de la Paix.
Olé in Spanish means the same as hooray.
In an airplane your food is served on a tray.
You may have to wait if there's a delay.
If you were a donkey, you could hee-haw and bray.
If you were a horse, you would whinny and neigh.
If you were a horse, you could also eat hay.
How long do you think this rhyme will stay?
Until the setting sun's last ray?

A MOOSE ON THE LOOSE

I saw a moose out driving,
speeding fast and far.
I asked, "Why are you driving
in a dashing motor car?"

The moose replied in moosy tones,
"I'll gladly tell you why:
I like these automatic brakes—
they happen to suit I."

The moose then said, "It's your turn now:
speak clearly and don't stammer."
I said to him, "Not *I* but *me*—
you'd better watch your grammar."

'Bye, fly.
Scat, cat.
Go, crow.
Begone, fawn.
Scram, lamb.
Vamoose, goose.
Hit the road, toad.
Jog, frog.
Out, trout.
Melt, smelt.
Whirl, squirrel.
Scoot, coot.
Get sunk, skunk.
Toodle-oo, kangaroo.

SCHENECTADY

Although I've been to Kankakee
and Kalamazoo and Kokomo,
the place I've always wanted to go,
the city I've always wanted to see
is Schenectady.

Schenectady, Schenectady,
though it's hard to pronounce correctly,
I plan to go there directly.

Schenectady, Schenectady,
yes, I want to connect with Schenectady,
the town I select is Schenectady,
I elect to go to Schenectady,
I'll take any trek to Schenectady,
even wash my neck for Schenectady,
so expect me next at Schenectady,
check and double-check
Schenectady!

Hands off the tablecloth
don't rumble belly
don't grab for grub
don't slurp the soup
don't crumble the crackers
don't mash the mushrooms
don't mush the potatoes
don't stab the steak
don't slap the saltshaker
don't pill the bread
don't swill the sauce
don't ooze the mayonnaise
don't slop the slaw
don't spatter the ketchup
don't gulp the olives
don't spit the pits
don't finger the lettuce
don't dribble dressing
don't chomp the celery
don't gobble the cobbler
don't guzzle the fizz
swallow, don't swig
don't smack your lips
pat with a napkin
daintily dab
quietly quaff
fastidious sip
and gracefully sample
a nibbling tidbit.

WHATNOT

I'm looking for my whatnot:
where can it be?

What is a whatnot?
It's plain as ABC.
It's not a thingumabob
or a jigamaree.

It's a whatnot that I've not got
and it belongs to me.

LEAK

Drip drips the kitchen faucet
drip in the sink plink plink
I'll plink you a new
of two who were true
and that is the drip of the plink.

Tap tap types the second-floor writer
It's late bangs the tenant above
Tap love tap story tap tap tum tum
tap never tap too tap late for love.

Drip drip drips the kitchen faucet
drip in the sink glub glub
drip drip night and day
there's glub to pay
and that is the rub of the glub.

Fellow blahs the candidate blab blahs
I promise to blah and blah more
you can trust in my blah if elected
my platform is worth blahing for.

Drip drip drip drips the kitchen faucet
tap blah glub plink drip drop tap drip plink
all things may stop
but not the drip drop
of the drip drip drip drip in the sink.

Drip drip drip

drip

d

r

i

p   *drip*

RUMMAGE

My mind is a catchall
of notions, ideas, sallies, a foray,
scribble a jotting—

like an attic trunk filled with junk:
hodgepodge of ragtag,
worn-out boots, buttons,
torn-pocketed vest, patchwork,
dog-eared stack of postcards, crumpled Christmas
   wrapping
twine tinsel tassels tangle snarl all knotted a snag of
ski-pole bathing suit bent hanger dangling
helter-skelter a clutter a scoop of pell-mell
beads beanbag hatbox wicker basket of
   higgledy-piggledy
throwcloth float-cushion scatter-rug hammock hassock
a jumble a stow
sloven of stash ravel of stickpin grabbag—

Order! Order! straighten out this disarray,
start filing, take inventory, build a shelf,
classify, sort, throw away!

And I promise myself I will
on the next rainy vacation day,
but my mind doesn't mind me;
saunters off in the rain
and slinks back with more to pack:

driftwood boat, lamp, table,
stone for a doorstop, stone for a paperweight,
and a gull's feather for tracing in sand
notions, ideas, and . . .

ARITHMETRIX

"Watch me juggle,
watch my tricks:
throw half a dozen
and then catch six.

"I can juggle time, too,"
the trickster speaks.
"Go for a fortnight
and return in two weeks."

TWO FROM THE ZOO

There is an animal known as a skink,
and no matter what you might happen to think
or ever have thunk,
a skink,
unlike a skunk,
does not stink.
A skink is a skink,
a reptilian slink.

If you go to the zoo
it may be on view
not far from an aye-aye.

Aye, yes, that's right.
Please take my word
that an aye-aye is not a sailor bird.
It's a bushy-tailed sight
that emerges at night.
Don't be afraid,
it won't start to wander,
it's not in the least
an unruly beast.

Truly
and zooly
two creatures to ponder.

VERSE PLAY

The poem's a ball
cupped in your hand,
open your fingers
and let it drop—

wait,
stop,

bounce it back
and catch the rhyme
just in time,
in time, in time.

A FISHY STORY

I saw a fish on Broadway
as finny as could be.
I asked, "Why are you here instead
of swimming in the sea?"

The fish replied, "My ego
is rather large, you see,
at sea I'm just another fish—
here people notice me.

"Now what," the fish then sneered at me,
"can you say that might be bright?"
"Cross at the green," I answered,
"and never against the light."

TRAVELING

Click, clack,
train on the track.

Conductor has to know
where you want to go.

Tap your toes,
tap, tap,
clap your hands,
clap, clap,
add a little ginger
with a finger snap.

Meet Sister Mattie
in Cincinnati,
Brother Ben
in Cheyenne.
Flip a coin in Des Moines.
Thanksgiving turkey
in Albuquerque,
eat red-hot beans
in New Orleans.
Pitch some hay in Santa Fe.
Lose a loose tooth
in Duluth,
open a store
in Baltimore.
Be noisy in Boise.
Nitty gritty

in New York City,
dance in a disco
in San Francisco.

Go, go, go, go.

Tap your toes,
tap, tap,
clap your hands,
clap, clap,
add a little ginger
with a finger snap.

Click, clack,
train on the track.

Full steam ahead
and don't look back.

ERASER

X
X
X
heed
my
hex:

I'll rub you out,
you'll disappear:
there goes your nose,
you've lost an ear,

your eyes are holes,
your chin is gone,
your neck and arms
have just passed on,

your knees melt down,
your feet are specks:
you're nothing but
an
ex
ex
ex!

QUIBBLE

U can be seen without a Q
but Q must always go with U.

I think it's queer
and not quite right.

So here is a Q all on its own.
Come on, Q. Stand up alone.
U keep out.

Alas, poor Q
feels qivery, qavery,
qietly sick . . .

Hurry back, U,
to the rescue—
quick!

MEAN SONG

Snickles and podes,
ribble and grodes:
that's what I wish you.

A nox in the groot,
a root in the stoot
and a gock in the forbeshaw, too.

Keep out of sight
for fear that I might
glom you a gravely snave.

Don't show your face
around anyplace
or you'll get one flack snack in the bave.

FIDDLE-FADDLE

Riddle me no,
riddle me yes,
what is the secret
of sweet success?

Said the razor, "Be keen."
"String along," said the bean.
"Push," said the door.
"Be polished," said the floor.
Said the piano, "Stand upright and grand."
"Be on the watch," said the second hand.

"Cool," said the ice cube.
"Bright," said the TV tube.
"Bounce back," said the yo-yo.
"Be well bred," said the dough.
"Plug," said the stopper.
"Shine," said copper.

"Be game," said the quail.
"Make your point," said the nail.
"Have patience," said the M.D.
"Look spruce," said the tree.
"Press on," said the stamp.
"Shed some light," said the lamp.
     "Oh, just have a good head,"
    the cabbage said.

THE BABY-SITTER AND THE BABY

Hush hush hush the baby-sitter sighs
waw! waw! waw! the little baby cries
Hush Hush shh shh Hush Hush Hush
    wawawwawwwwwww
       hush hush
          waw waw
             hush hush
             WAW!

Ah ooh ooh the baby-sitter tries
snuggle you and huggle you gently ooh ah ooh
Naw naw naw the baby cries and cries
      hush hush
         waw waw
        ooh ooh
          NAW!

Lulla lulla lulla lull you lullabies
sleepy sleepy sleepy
deepy dreamy lullabies
please will you please please please shut your eyes
YiYiYi the baby cries and cries
   hush hush
      waw waw
        ooh ooh
          naw naw
            lulla lulla
              yi yi
            yi
        yi
        YI!

ASSOCIATIONS

Home to me is not a house
filled with family faces.

Home is where I slide in free
by rounding all the bases.

A tie to me is not
clothing like a hat.

It means the game is even up
and I wish I were at bat.

SPRING FEVER

Danny dawdles
Sally shilly-shallies
Lloyd loiters
Guy gambols
Sylvia saunters
Peter procrastinates
Amanda meanders
Leonard lingers
Samuel ambles
Dorothy dallies
Harry tarries
and Molly lolls.

FAST FOOD

Stab a slab,
nab a dab,
munch,
crunch,
slurp,
burp,
grab the tab.

THE STUCK HORN

unmOOOOOOOOOOOOOOOOOving
in glUUUUUUUUUUUUUUUUUUUUe

sunk in OOOOOOOOOOOOOOOOOOOze
snaggling in the same dragging
grOOOOOOOOOOOOOOOOOOOOOOOOOOOOOve

throw a bOOOOOOOOOOOOOOOt or a shOOOe
gag it with a rag   bottle it   stopple it   pickle it
pinprick it   tickle it with a straw from a
brOOOOOOOOOOOOOOOOOOOOOOOOOOOOOm

just when you think it will stop, it
reneWWWWWWWWWWWWWWWWWWWWW
    WWWWWWWWWWWWWWWWWWWWs

somebody please
dOOOOOOOOOOOOOOOOOOOOOOOOO
something sOOOOOOOOOOOOOOOOOOOOOOOOOOO
    OOOOOOOOOOOOOOOOOOn

GEOGRAPHY

You can ride for long treks
in *Tex.* and *N. Mex.*

Skyscrapers high
in *N.Y.*

Fish
in *Mich.*

Tomatoes in *N.J.*
Flowers in *Va.*
Coal in *Pa.*, and rice in *La.*

Cotton in *Ala.*
Okra in *Okla.*

Corn grows in *O.*,
Ia., and *Mo.*

Lumber in *Minn.*
In *Mont.* there's tin.

Chickens in *R.I.*
Cattle in *Wy.*
Hunter's pie in *Ky.*

Fla. beaches,
Ga. peaches.

Wash. grows pears,
Colo. has bears.

Shoes come from *Mass.*,
salmon from *Alas.*

Cal., redwood trees,
Wis. is known for cheese.

Mushrooms in *Del.*
Conn., Christmas trees to sell.

Kans. sows wheat,
Ill. ships meat.

Green hills in *Vt.*
Now that's enough from *Me.*

Seventeen states more I leave
For *U.* to abbreve.

TUBE TIME

I turned on the TV
and what did I see?

I saw a can of cat food talking,
a tube of toothpaste walking.

> Peanuts, popcorn,
> cotton flannel.
> Jump up, jump up,
> switch the channel.

I turned to Station B
and what did I see?

I saw a shampoo bottle crying,
a pile of laundry flying.

> Peanuts, popcorn,
> cotton flannel.
> Jump up, jump up,
> switch the channel.

I turned to Station D
and what did I see?

I saw two spray cans warring,
a cup of coffee snoring.

Peanuts, popcorn,
cotton flannel.
Jump up, jump up,
switch the channel.

I turned to Station E
and what did I see?

I saw dancing fingers dialing,
an upset stomach smiling.

Peanuts, popcorn,
cotton flannelette.
Jump up, jump up
turn off the set.

ULULATION

With a bray, with a yap,
with a grunt, snort, neigh,
with a growl, bark, yelp,
with a buzz, hiss, howl,
with a chirrup, mew, moo,
with a snarl, baa, wail,
with a blatter, hoot, bay,
with a screech, drone, yowl,
with a cackle, gaggle, guggle,
with a chuck, cluck, clack,
with a hum, gobble, quack,
with a roar, blare, bellow,
with a yip, croak, crow,
with a whinny, caw, low,
with a bleat, with a cheep, with a squawk, with a
  squeak:

animals
  —and sometimes humans—
                  speak!

SUPERMARKET, SUPERMARKET
(A Jump Rope Rhyme)

Supermarket, supermarket,
shelves piled high
with brand-new products
for you to buy:

vegetable soap flakes,
filter-tip milk,
frozen chicken wings ready to fly,

shreddable edible paper towels,
banana detergent,
deodorant pie.

METHUSELAH

Methuselah, Methuselah.
So long-lived a man was he,
the candles on his birthday cake
lit all the ships at sea!

Methuselah, that longevity man,
had a long, *long*, LONG white beard
that started to grow in Canada
and in Florida still appeared!

Methuselah, that high old-timer,
never was one for tears;
he thought the world was a funny place—
and laughed for a thousand years!

That millennium man might be living yet,
and he'd write this instead of me,
except that one day he kicked up his heels
and rocked himself with glee;

for it struck him as the funniest sight
that people on earth were so queer:
with only two legs and only two arms
and only two ears to hear,

with less than three eyes in each single head,
it was strange as strange could be;
they all looked so very much alike
in the human family

you could scarcely tell one from another
compared to outer-space faces,
and their world was so small compared to all
interplanetary places,

and yet they fought among themselves:
imagine such idiocy?
That antic antique laughed himself sick
and soon died of hilarity.

A WORD OR TWO WITH YOU

The sound of *must*
reeks of indoors
shut up with homework and chores

whereas
volunteer
packs up camping gear
and mountain views
that say Wishyouwerehere.

THE
SINGING
GREEN

SECRET HAND

I closed my eyes
and made a fist of my hand:

I held a stripe
from the tiger tree,
an emerald snowflake,
a drop of orange rain,
and thirteen purple
grains of sand.

Then
I opened my fingers
and I let them
fly free.

FROM THE JAPANESE

The summer night
is a dark blue hammock
slung between the white pillars of day.

I lie there
cooling myself
with the straw-colored
flat round fan
of the full moon.

RUBY-THROATED HUMMINGBIRD

Where?
   there!
         scarlet needle-dart
skimming the air
         vermilion flick
               red startle

flitter
     heartbeat flutter
            shutter openingclosing
               clickclick

flare up   flicker   flurry hurry
              hairsbreadth
too late   flame's blown out
        flown on.

WAYS OF COMPOSING

typewriter
a mouthful of teeth chattering
afraid to be quiet

a pencil can lie down and dream
dark and silver silences

HURRY

Hurry! says the morning,
don't be late for school!

Hurry! says the teacher,
hand in papers now!

Hurry! says the mother,
supper's getting cold!

Hurry! says the father,
time to go to bed!

Slowly, says the darkness,
you can talk to me . . .

SILENCE

Quiet,
so quiet
without a sound

floating,
falling
to the ground

snowflake feathers
from snow-white birds

snow is a poem
without any words.

BY THE SEA

Morning
I run with the sea:
together we break
the tape of land.

Noon
Emerald flames leap high,
are quenched;
the embers barely stir . . .
a moment later,
fire,
green fire!

Night
Beyond mortality,
the sea:
a wild dark shout,
a pale dying out,
the combers flying, then homing,
flying, homing,
over and ever again.

THREE STRANGENESSES
OF EVERY DAY

To fall asleep
to dream
to awaken

RAINBOW WRITING

Nasturtiums with
their orange cries
flare like trumpets;
their music dies.

Golden harps
of butterflies;
the strings are mute
in autumn skies.

Vermilion chords,
then silent gray;
the last notes of
the song of day.

Rainbow colors
fade from sight,
come back to me
when I write.

SOLITUDE

Solitude
is a mood to share
with the last day of autumn,
with the last leaf that falls,
with the last tree bare

and below is the root,
the silent root

that will bear through the dark
through the cold
through the storm,

that will bear
seed   bud   and fruit
to the flowering air.

GRANDMOTHER, ROCKING

Last night I dreamed of an old lover,
I had not seen him in forty years.
When I awoke,
I saw him on the street:
his hair was white,
his back stooped.
How could I say hello?
He would have been puzzled all day
about who the young girl was
who smiled at him.
So I let him go on his way.

DECIDUOUS

Deciduous deciduous
dying fall
deciduous deciduous
lorn lorn
last leaf torn
deciduous deciduous
perishing all.
  Maple elm sycamore
    birch beech mountain ash
      poplar linden tamarack
        oak come back come back come back

      crimson gold turned widow's weed
     orchard lane meadow field
   gone to weed   to buried seed

Deciduous deciduous
dark months mourn
deciduous deciduous
spare spare
black bough bare
deciduous deciduous

Spring reborn.

EVERGREEN

Hemlock and pine
stand in July
grassy steeples
against the sky.

Sequoia and yew
October days short
green shadows lengthen
over the court.

Spruce and cypress
December winds blow
emerald palaces
shining in snow.

Cedar and fir
March freshets and rains
whatever the season
green remains.

Juniper conifer constancy
evergreen evergreen evergreen grow
evergreen evergreen ever green grow.

THE FLYING PEN

I am looking for a book
I do not know its title
or what it is about

but if I find it
and turn to the right page

it will read me

it will put a pen into my hands
that will sprout iridescent feathers
and fly.

THE STRAY CAT

It's just an old alley cat
that has followed us all the way home.

It hasn't a star on its forehead,
or a silky satiny coat.

No proud tiger stripes, no dainty tread,
no elegant velvet throat.

It's a splotchy, blotchy
city cat, not pretty cat,
a rough little tough little bag of old bones.

What shall we call this
city cat, not pretty cat,
this rough little tough little bag of old bones?

"Beauty," we shall call you,
"Beauty, come in."

STARRY NIGHT I

Crescendo!
A million notes of music fly off the printed page
  in a melodic rage.
Brass, woodwinds, strings, percussion
all blare forth their orchestra of light
onto the nighttime stage.

STARRY NIGHT II

The night flowers for me,
as though the dew of every petal of every dawn
  has shaken free.
I swim in the skybloom sea.

ICE-CREEPERS

"Aren't you fearful you'll trip and fall?"
I asked the old lady out walking alone,
alone on the snow-covered path.

"No," she said, "I've my ice-creepers on,
metal prongs on the soles of my shoes;
they dig in and grip."
She lifted one heel so that bits of steel flashed
in the zero-round sun.
"Besides, if I break a hip or a leg,
I'm old enough to be long gone tripping
on my own grave.
Being afraid is for those
with the winter road all still ahead.
It's the young you should worry for
who may be sent to war or die
out of a job, out in the cold.
I'll keep on getting along."
Then she put her foot down and went stamping on
with the rest of her ice-creeping song:

"ching ching
cling cling
the metal prongs make a nice chirpy sound
over the frozen ground
ching ching
cling cling
crunching the ice
like twigs

like flowering sprigs
like the crunchable bones of small baby birds
and brittle old loners like me
ching ching
cling cling
all the way down
to the hold in the open sea."

DREAM VOYAGE TO THE CENTER
OF THE SUBWAY

One day
the billboards all implore
"BUY NOTHING"

In the broken vending machine
push the plunger
and pop out
a flower
sprung dewborn
fresh every hour.

SOMEDAY

Someday wooed a peacock,
Monday thought of molt;
Someday flung the window,
Tuesday drew the bolt.

Wednesday dried the dishes,
Someday dribbled juice;
Thursday counted dollar bills,
Someday's coins cut loose.

Friday wore a raincoat,
Someday splashed the boss;
Saturday looked to and fro,
Someday leaped across.

Ah oneday come moonday
come chooseday   come whensday
my hersday   my freeday
my satyrday SUN!

THE OPTILEAST AND
THE PESSIMOST

The Optileast
is a cheerful beast;
the least little thing
makes joy bells ring.

The Pessimost
is given to boast
that there's always room
for more and more gloom.

Now these two creatures, queer to relate,
whom nature would scarcely be able to mate;
who neither the other could ever abide,
who surely could never live side by side—
queer as can be, although they're not kin,
they dwell within the very same skin.

Times when my Optileast is here,
my Pessimost does not appear,
and yet she's somewhere down below
even though she does not show;
so do not be alarmed or shout
if she should suddenly break out.

Then when my Pessimost is seen
and acting bigly mean as mean;
without any warning in advance,
my Optileast begins to dance:
the smallest flower, or nothing at all,
can make her leap up laughing tall.

Strange Optileast and Pessimost,
neither is guest, neither is host;
they couldn't be sisters, they couldn't be wed,
yet they'll live together until they're dead.
For however peculiar it may be,
they're both alive, alive in me.

THE WHOLLY FAMILY

Baby's got a plastic bottle,
plastic pacifier to chew;
plastic pillows on the sofa,
plastic curtains frame the view;
plastic curlers do up Mama,
Mama's hairdo's plastic, too.

Junior plays with plastic modules,
Sister pins on plastic bows;
plastic wallet made for Papa,
plastic credit cards in rows;
plastic ivy in the planter
greener than the real thing grows.

Plastic pumpkin for Thanksgiving,
plastic beach ball by the sea;
plastic snow at Christmastime,
plastic manger, star, and tree;
plastic used so totally
keeps us germproof and dirt-free.

Praise of plastic thus we sing,
plastic over everything
keeps us cool and safe and dry:
it may not pain us much to die.

COUNTRY CALENDAR

Tendril green unfurls to rose,
crimson leaves lie under snows;
the seasons change, the year bestows
green   rose   crimson   white
constant flow of new delight.

WHERE IS A POEM?

Where is a poem?
As far away
as a rainbow span,
ancient Cathay,
or Afghanistan;

or it can be near
as where you stand
this very day
on Main Street here
with a poem
in your hand.

What makes a poem?
Whatever you feel:
the secrets of rain
on a windowpane,
the smell of a rose
or of cowboy clothes,
the sound of a flute
or a foghorn hoot,
the taste of cake
or a freshwater lake,
the touch of grass
or an icy glass,
the shout of noon
or the silent moon,
a standstill leaf
or a rolling wheel,
laughter and grief:
whatever you feel.

SUMMER SOLSTICE

Full-blown blooms the dewsprung morning,
honeyed clings afternoon,
golden flows the eventide,
and no dark side to the moon.

THE HILL

Three of us here on the hill,
free as the breezes that blow;
we could stay here forever on top of the world
and never go back to the valley below.

Tom, free from his sick mother's whine
(only the wind in the pine),
her twitching cheek, her palsied hands,
her paralyzing demands.

Ann, free from her fixed everyday
(the clouds shift every which way),
in a box of a room with a steel-gray file
and a permanent plastic smile.

Myself, beyond the shadows of doubt
(the air is clear all about),
having to plan my own life ahead,
half wishing I still could be led.

Three of us here on the hill,
free as the breezes that blow;
we could stay here forever on top of the world:
we start our descent to the valley below.

SOUVENIR

I bring back a shell so I can always hear
the music of the ocean when I hold it to my ear:

then I feel again the grains of sand
trickle sun-warm through my hand

the sea gulls dip and swoop and cry
as they dive for fish then climb the sky

the sailboats race with wings spread wide
as the wind spins them round and they glide ride
   glide

my lips taste a crust of salty foam
and sandpipers skitter and crabs scuttle home

where I build a castle of Yesterday
that the high tide washes away away

while I keep the shell so I can always hear
the music of the ocean when I hold it to my ear.

TALKING TO THE SUN

Do you like to shine all the time?
Do you ever feel you are too much in the light?
Are you cool toward the moon?
Distant to the stars?
Do you wish you could be taller in winter?

ON BEING INTRODUCED TO YOU

Cinquain:
five lines, unrhymed;
start with two syllables,
go to four, six, eight, but at length
just two.

No watch
can tell love's time:
the hour is always
unbidden, when least expected,
as now.

Joy comes
as a light craft
darting on the surface
of the sea, then dropping anchor
to stay.

WHEN

When fire's freezing cold,
when snow is boiling hot,
when birds forget to sing,
I'll still forget you not.

When every story ends,
when spring does not renew,
when all the clocks have stopped,
will I stop loving you?

SAY NAY

What is true for me and you
is that it ticks inexorably with time:

say nay
and fear each year

always on the knife-edge of life
as close as breath to death

landscape where if you choose a leaf
grief ensues

no song lasts long
a flower fades in an hour

love is a mourning dove
all trust turns to rust

and tomorrow
leads straight to sorrow

but balance on the tightrope of hope
and what's sad becomes glad

the stain of pain
washes away in rain

a perfect rose
grows

praise of days
when there is mirth upon earth

cheer here
bless yes

and live with laughter happily ever after.

LOVE LETTERS, UNMAILED

Your hand
brushes my hair
and little bells
jump
in the air startling
me so that I
cling to you for fear of
falling up into the sky.

The touch of
your fingers
grazing mine
delicate as
a single drop of wine
in a crystal goblet.
Rolling it round,
I savor it
on my tongue,
try to
make it last
forever.

The words
I
love
you
form
in the air
and melt.

Your palm
against
my cheek,
light as
a snowflake.

PROSE AND POETRY

You can be immersed in good prose, like swimming
in a lake on a warm summer afternoon.

In poetry
the ice-cold moon
drops down
into the lake,
melts
to surround you,
and then
together
you fly back home
to the sky.

GIFT WRAPPING

Tear off a sheet
of dark blue paper

the kind with
ragged edges of gray

fold it in
so the edges don't show

then from a ball
of gilt twine

snip off
just length enough

to loop around
and tie a knot and bow

now pull at one end of the bow
it opens easily

it opens up
into morning sunfire blazing blue.

POINTS OF THE COMPASS

West is the springtime:
infinite beckoning;

farther, reach farther,
sky will be bluer;

farther, reach farther,
earth shall be fairer;

farther reach farther:
fool's-gold frontier.

South is the summer:
a barefoot road leads
to firefly screen doors,
day-lily weeds,
to the moon in the pond,
a voice in the reeds.

Gorge on ripe melon,
scatter the seeds.

East is the autumn:
harvest is binned;
sit round the fire
banked from the wind;

stare at the flames,
at leaping desire . . .
smoldering ashes,
who'll prod the fire?

North is the winter:
the long polar night

facelessly noplace
ghostghastly sight

cold as a blank page
endlessly white

till penguins appear
for a line of black type.

THE POEM AS A DOOR

A door
is never
either/or.
A door
is always
more.

You cannot skip over,
you cannot crawl under;
walk through the wood,
it splits asunder.

If you expect it to be bolted,
it will be.

There is only one opening:
yourself as the key.

With a sigh of happiness
you pass through
to find on the other side
someone with a sigh of happiness
welcoming you.

PIGEONS

Other birds soar in the clouds

these are city dwellers
they see the sky
only between clumps of buildings

they nest on fire escapes
air conditioners
basement stoops

they can nest on nails

they are gray and bedraggled
they flap their wings in the midst of filth
and they make more filth

they are noisy
they are disgusting
they have an iridescent beauty

they huddle   they survive

AS THE GUNS THUNDER

As the guns thunder,
as the bombs blast,
as the bullets of history
go whining past

as the heart drums,
as the bugles call,
let the lying names for War
be heard above all:

Necessity
      Defense
            Victory

REPLY TO THE QUESTION:
"How Can You Become a Poet?"

take the leaf of a tree
trace its exact shape
the outside edges
and inner lines

memorize the way it is fastened to the twig
(and how the twig arches from the branch)
how it springs forth in April
how it is panoplied in July

by late August
crumple it in your hand
so that you smell its end-of-summer sadness

chew its woody stem

listen to its autumn rattle

watch as it atomizes in the November air

then in winter
when there is no leaf left
                    invent one

THE FABLE OF THE GOLDEN PEAR

Once, upon fair fortune's tree,
there grew a golden pear;
and as is fairly common there,
wishes were granted three.

The first flung by
with a covetous eye:
"Oh, that all alone I might
for a quickening hour taste delight!"
But single self could scarce begin,
could merely nibble the outer skin.

Who clutches at a lonely feast
must sour leave before the sweet;
for such is the gift of the golden pear,
such is the power of love to share.

The second reined by
with a prudent eye:
"I dearly long to bite deeper in,
but juice might stain my spotless chin;
I could only afford to enjoy it if
I were neatly wearing a handkerchief."

Who wants for more inclining time
will savor nothing of the feast;
for such is the gift of the golden pear,
such is the power of love to dare.

The third came by
with an eager eye:
      "Right ruddy in reach by the highway side,
      fit for a king of the world and his bride—
      and who can that more certainly be
      than the likes of present company?"

      Consumed, and golden grew again.
      For one who most unsparing cares:
      the pear will never disappear,
      the power of love is always here.

SKYWRITING

1.
Fireworks!
They shower down as verbs,
and come to rest as nouns.

Fountain in reverse,
words that delight take flight,
flash like fireworks in the air,
blazon and remain there.

2.
Adjectives like leaves
palpitate the trees.
Yearly the seasons must renew
as April's green and singing sound
falls to silent winter ground.

A poem shapes the landscape,
holds the singing green.
Leaves that do not die,
planted in the poem sky.

3.
Birds write verses in the sky:
swift verbs that fly,
slow nouns in their downy nest.
Wingbeat repeat, repeat
the symmetry of birds, of words.

The flight soaring,
the song outpouring.
The flight dying,
the song still flying.